Why We Are in Need of Tales

Part IV

Why We Are in Need of Tales

Part IV

discovering philosophical treasures in picture books

Maria daVenza Tillmanns

Published by Iguana Books
720 Bathurst Street, Suite 303
Toronto, ON M5S 2R4

Publisher: Cheryl Hawley
Editor: Holly Warren
Front cover image: Diego Gonzales
Back cover image: Nevaeh Hernandez
All drawings used with the permission of the artists and their parent(s).

ISBN 978-77180-624-4 (hardcover)
ISBN 978-77180-623-7 (paperback)
ISBN 978-77180-622-0 (ebook)

This is an original print edition of *Why We Are in Need of Tales, Part IV.*

To those who live life on life's terms

How to deal with what is beyond our control

A very, very long time ago, we used to have tails. These tails connected us to the world around us and to each other. We used them to communicate, and they let us do so with incredible accuracy and nuance — with the slightest twitch of the tail, we could communicate our deepest thoughts and feelings. Imagine!

But as time went on, we started to lose our tails. They became shorter and shorter and shorter until they disappeared altogether. And with their disappearance, we lost that mysterious connection to our world and to each other.

Why We Are in Need of Tails introduces us to Huk and Tuk, who discover that telling each other tales can help us reconnect to the mystery called life. Huk and Tuk discover that telling each other tales brings back a sense of wonder — and it is this sense of wonder that helps us reconnect with each other and to the world around us. In the tales Huk and Tuk tell each other, they wonder about what it means to be fair, or to be a friend, or to have willpower. They find out it is also possible to wonder about what is on the other side of a wall — any wall — and to expand their vision using imagination. They find out that wondering, and especially wondering together, helps to keep the spark of life alive — even when life is challenging and there are no clear answers.

In *Why We Are in Need of Tales*, Part I, Huk and Tuk share tales with each other and unearth the philosophical treasures buried within them.

In Part II, these two best friends discuss more tales — this time with a focus on the importance of dreams. They find that dreams, which seem to come out of nowhere, reconnect us by sparking our curiosity and our imagination. Huk and Tuk, by the way, also materialized out of nowhere — a very creative place in infinite space; a place that's everywhere and nowhere at the same time.

In Part III, Huk and Tuk tell each other tales about how our decisions can help us make our dreams come true. You may wonder how decisions can possibly do that, though. Well, when we simply follow along and don't think much about why we are doing one thing instead of another thing, we're making decisions with our eyes half closed, really, and may not see the opportunities to make our dreams come true. Huk and Tuk have learned that we need to keep our eyes wide open when we venture through life, much like we do when we wander through the woods.

And finally, in this book, *Why We Are in Need of Tales*, Part IV, Huk and Tuk discuss how to deal with the things in life that are beyond our control. There are many — so, so many — situations in life that are not in our control, yet we have to deal with them one way or another. But how, and on what basis, do we make our decisions in *those* situations? In these next tales, Huk and Tuk discuss what lies at the basis of the decisions we need to make when things are beyond our control. Huk and Tuk know that this is a very tough subject and that without some kind of deep connection to the world around us and to each other, it is nearly impossible to deal with these kinds of situations.

What it means to be brave when faced with what is beyond our control

— *Dragons and Giants* by Arnold Lobel —

Huk and Tuk sat on Tuk's back porch one afternoon, sipping the apple juice they had made together with the apples from the trees below Huk's house.

You know, said Tuk, tales have a way of making you wiser. Huk and Tuk always enjoyed sharing wonderful, full-of-wonder tales with each other, but this was a new idea to contemplate.

Wiser? asked Huk. How so?

Well, Tuk said, I think tales get you to think about things differently. I think they can even make you think about life differently.

Tales teach us, Tuk continued, that what we think we know, we really don't know.

Kind of like Socrates said? Huk asked. Tuk looked puzzled. You know, Socrates, the famous Greek philosopher? He said that too, continued Huk, but I don't think he was talking about how *tales* make you wiser. Anyway, how do tales make us realize that what we think we know, we don't really know?

Well, Tuk began, remember the tale about the missing piece? Remember how we thought the pie-like something — oh, remember how we called her Sandy? — would be delighted when she finally found her missing piece? But then, to our surprise, she ended up putting the missing piece down and continued her life without it. She felt more complete without her missing piece than with it. That makes you think, doesn't it?

That's true, Huk said. I think most of us would have thought that happiness is a result of being perfect or complete, or something like that.

Yeah, Tuk said, but then Sandy learned that life is not about being perfect; it's about relationships, really. After she found her missing piece, Sandy rolled past them so fast that she missed out on talking with the worm, smelling a flower and seeing the butterflies. She had no time for them anymore. So she decided to continue her life without the missing piece — and she felt more perfect without it. See, Sandy first thought she'd be happier *with* the missing piece, but then when she had found it, she learned she was actually much happier without it.

Oh, I get it, said Huk, she learned that what she thought she knew — that she would be happier with her missing piece — she didn't know, and she was actually happier without it.

That's true, Tuk agreed.

I know a tale about Frog and Toad wanting to know whether they were really brave or not, Tuk said. After looking in the mirror and wondering whether they *looked* brave, they decided they would have to find out if they really were brave by *actually* climbing the mountain just outside Toad's house. They wanted to find out what they thought might be true was really true, because Frog and Toad figured out that *thinking* they may be brave and possibly *looking* brave didn't by any means indicate whether they were *in fact* brave.

Or foolish, Huk interrupted. Remember the tale about Doctor De Soto and his wife and the fox? It wasn't clear in that tale whether the De Sotos were *actually* brave by letting the fox into their dentistry or if they were maybe just foolish. Even Doctor De Soto thought it was foolish to have trusted a fox and to have let him in!

Although, Huk continued, the De Sotos *did* realize the danger involved in letting the fox in — twice. It's not that they had their eyes closed. That would have made them foolish, I think. In fact, they had their eyes wide open and decided to help the fox anyway. They helped him because he was in pain, not because he was a fox, an animal that could be very, very dangerous to mice like the De Sotos.

Okay, Tuk replied, that does make sense. So, someone is foolish if they are not aware of the danger involved? But you can't always *be aware* of exactly the danger you are in. There's always something that is beyond your control.

So, what happened to Frog and Toad? Huk wanted to know. Were they aware of any possible danger they would face climbing the mountain? Or was it foolish of them to test their bravery that way?

Well, you tell me, Tuk said.

Frog and Toad started to climb the mountain, Tuk continued. This was going to be their test to prove to themselves whether they were a brave frog and a brave toad or not.

They knew it might be dangerous but did not know what kind of danger they would be in. That was beyond their control.

So, Tuk said, everything was going smoothly as they climbed the mountain. Then they came to a dark cave and — suddenly — a snake came out of the cave and said, Hello lunch. The snake opened his mouth wide.

Oh no! Huk exclaimed. Frog and Toad would make a delicious lunch for that snake.

It's okay, Tuk said. Frog and Toad jumped out of the way *just* in time. Toad was shaking like a leaf and tried to sound brave. He cried out, I'm not afraid!

After that first scare, they continued their journey up the mountain.

It's brave of them to continue climbing the mountain instead of running back home, Huk said.

by Kyeann Ogalino

Tuk nodded and kept going. They climbed on and heard a loud noise and then many large stones came rolling down the mountain.

Toad cried out, It's an avalanche! Frog and Toad jumped out of the way *just* in time.

Frog trembled and tried to sound brave, shouting, I'm not afraid!

They are being tested on this hike up the mountain, Huk said. These are dangerous encounters. Poor Frog and Toad must be scared stiff even though they don't want to admit it, of course, shouting instead that they are not afraid.

Did they go back home after that? Huk asked. I would have!

No, Tuk said, they went *all the way* up to the top of the mountain.

That means they are brave, Huk concluded. I would have called it a day — brave or not — and gone back home.

The tale continues with Frog and Toad suddenly seeing the shadow of a hawk overhead, and they both jumped under a rock *just* in time. The hawk

by Carlos Dominguez

flew away. We're not afraid, they both screamed. And they started running down the mountain as fast as they could. They ran and ran and ran until they finally got to Toad's house.

So, they got home safe? Huk wanted to know.

Yes, and then Toad jumped into his bed and pulled the covers over his head and Frog jumped into the closet and shut the door. And they stayed there for a very long time.

Being scared doesn't mean you're not brave, Huk decided. It means being able to carry on even though you are scared. So then do you have to be somewhat scared in order to be brave?

I think so, Tuk replied, because being scared is being scared of something beyond your control. I mean, Frog and Toad were not in control of the snake, who was looking for lunch, or the avalanche that was coming their way, or the hawk that swooped down.

That's interesting, isn't it? said Huk. I think we often think that being brave means not being scared of something, but that's not it at all.

And, Tuk continued, if Frog and Toad were not afraid at all, they may not have jumped out of the way of the snake, the avalanche or the hawk. They obviously had their eyes wide open to avert the danger they were in and continue their journey up the mountain.

Even though they were really scared, Huk commented, it didn't stop them from going all the way up the mountain. So, in my opinion, Frog and Toad found out they were in fact brave. They were brave in their encounters with what was way out of their control. What do you think?

Tuk agreed, I think Frog and Toad are one brave frog and one brave toad.

by Jessica Leon

How to deal with the forces of nature beyond our control

— *The Garden* by Arnold Lobel —

The next day Tuk went over to Huk's house and, as always, was impressed with how well Huk tended the front garden. Tuk was amazed at the many flowers and shrubs and bushes. Tuk could see that Huk gave the garden a lot of care and attention.

It's rather wild, Tuk thought, but it all looks so perfectly imperfect, or — and Tuk smiled — imperfectly perfect.

Huk came outside to greet Tuk, and together they quietly enjoyed the garden for several minutes.

Huk then asked if Tuk knew the funny story about how his best friend's beautiful garden made Toad want a garden of his own.

Tuk wasn't surprised to hear this, since Tuk had been having similar thoughts about Huk's garden.

Huk started telling the story. It's hard work, Frog told Toad. But here are some seeds. Put these seeds in the ground and that way you can start your garden.

Tuk, not being quite sure how gardens work exactly, asked, What happened next?

Toad took the seeds and ran home. He carefully created a flowerbed the way Frog had shown him and planted the flower seeds.

Then Toad instructed the seeds to grow. Now seeds, Toad said, start growing!

Toad walked up and down the flowerbed, hoping the seeds would start growing, but he didn't see any change.

Did Toad *really* think that the seeds would start growing the minute he put them in the ground? Even Tuk knew that it took more time and patience than that!

Obviously, Toad had no clue, Huk said. Toad then put his head close to the ground and raised his voice, NOW SEEDS, START GROWING!

Alas, said Huk, as you may have expected, the seeds did *not* start to grow. Tuk nodded, trying

by Samantha Ceballos

to demonstrate that he knew that's not how it works.

Toad tried again and raised his voice even more, practically yelling at the seeds to start growing. At this point, Frog, hearing all the noise, went over to Toad's house.

What is going on here? Frog asked.

My seeds won't grow, Toad said, sounding exasperated.

They are afraid to grow, said Frog. Leave them alone for a couple of days. Let the sun shine and the rain fall on them. Then they will start to grow.

That night, Toad looked out the window and saw that his seeds still had not started to grow. Then Toad thought, If my seeds are afraid to grow, maybe it's because they're afraid of the dark. So, he took candles out to the garden with him and put them in the ground. He read the seeds a story by candlelight, hoping they would not be afraid.

And so, Huk continued, Toad sang, read poems and played his violin for his seeds.

Tuk interrupted, Toad plays the violin?

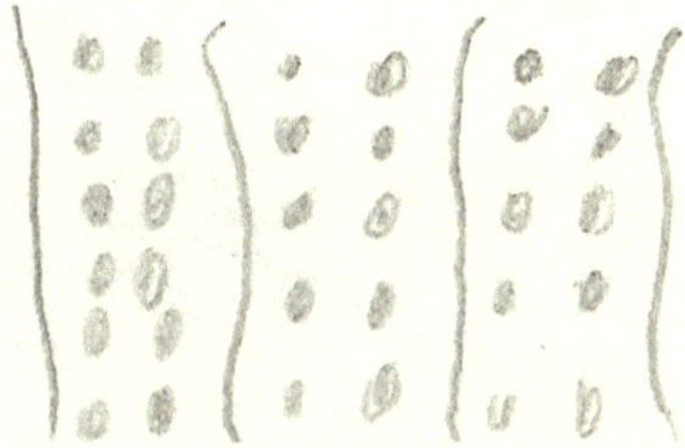

by Roberto Camacho

by Kyeann Ogalino

I didn't know that either, said Huk and then continued, Eventually Toad got very tired and fell asleep next to his seeds. He slept for a long time.

When Frog showed up to see how Toad was doing, he found his friend fast asleep. Frog nudged Toad awake and said, Look Toad, look at your garden.

And guess what, Tuk — tiny shoots had started to come out of the ground!

Toad was overjoyed and said, My seeds stopped being afraid and finally decided to start growing! But Toad also agreed that having a garden was really hard work.

Do you think Toad learned anything about growing a garden?

Well, Tuk replied, Frog did tell Toad growing a garden was hard work. And, I guess, Toad figured that meant *doing* something, like singing to the seeds, and reading poems and playing his violin. See, that's all hard work to Toad.

And sitting around doing nothing — just waiting for the seeds to grow — is not particularly hard work, is it?

Tuk could see how Toad was confused. Waiting for seeds to grow is not hard work, Tuk conceded.

So, what does make it hard work, then? Tuk asked.

We cannot force seeds to grow, said Huk. That's beyond our control. We can create conditions for them to grow, but the seeds do their own growing in their own time.

Maybe Toad learned that to grow a garden is to let *the garden* do the growing. I mean, said Tuk, we cannot do the growing *for* the seeds. That's out of our control.

And, said Huk, we're only now slowly learning that nature has its own way of doing things, after we've thought for so long that we can control it. Well, when we still had tails, because our tails connected us to nature, we knew we had no control over nature, but somehow we forgot it again when we lost our tails.

Tuk laughed and said, So we now have to learn what Toad had to learn — that we cannot control what is beyond our control. Isn't that some profound insight!

by Isabella Cervantes

Huk laughed and said, Tales do have a way of getting us to see things in a new way — in a way we had not thought of before. Or sometimes, I think they even reveal the obvious and get us to see what was there but had not been considered before.

How to accept things when they get out of control

— *A New House* by Arnold Lobel —

Below Huk's house are a lot of apple trees. In fall, Huk and Tuk go down there to pick apples to bring home and bake apple pie — *delicious* apple pie.

While they were picking apples one day, Tuk looked up at the trees and asked Huk, Remember our friend Grasshopper? Did you know he ran into a *lot of* trouble one day all because of *an apple*?

What happened? Huk asked.

Grasshopper climbed to the top of a steep hill, Tuk said, and he was quite hungry when he got all the way up there. He spotted a large apple lying on the ground, so he decided to take a big bite out of it.

But Worm lived in that apple and cried out to Grasshopper, Look what you did! Now there is a big hole in my roof.

Oh no! Grasshopper thought. I am so sorry, Grasshopper told Worm. But before he could

by Fawad Fnu

finish apologizing, the apple started rolling down the hill.

That sure doesn't sound good, said Huk.

Worm cried out in a panic, Tuk continued, pleading with Grasshopper to stop the apple from rolling down the hill.

Poor Grasshopper ran after the apple, but the apple started rolling faster and faster and Grasshopper could not do anything to stop it.

Grasshopper heard Worm, who was totally upset, cry out, Help! Please!

Worm's head was bumping on the walls! His dishes were falling off the shelf. Everything turned into a complete mess!

Can you imagine? Tuk said. His bathtub was in the living room! His bed was in the kitchen!

The situation only got worse and worse, Tuk continued.

Grasshopper kept running. This situation was way beyond his control. He did not know what else to do to stop the apple from rolling and rolling and rolling. Grasshopper could not catch up.

The apple rolled all the way down the hill. At

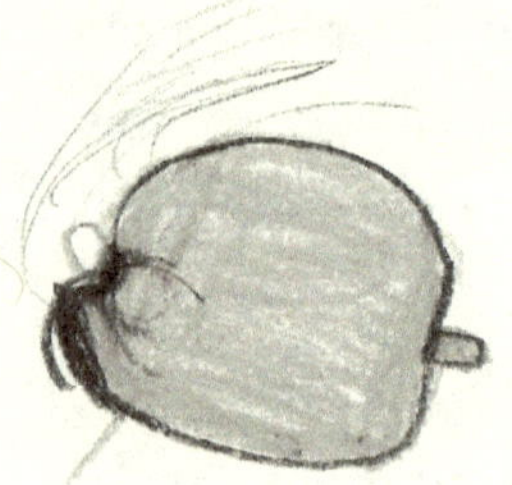

by Abraham Ponce

the bottom of the hill, the apple — namely Worm's house — smashed into a tree and was destroyed. Grasshopper wasn't sure what to say, so he blurted out the obvious: Your house is gone!

Worm must have been really angry at Grasshopper, Huk said. Imagine if *your* house had smashed apart.

That's the interesting thing, Tuk replied. I don't think Worm *was* angry. Rather, he appreciated that Grasshopper made a real effort to try and save his house.

Worm knew that after Grasshopper had taken a bite out of the apple, the situation just got way out of control.

And Grasshopper knew that he hadn't meant to hurt Worm. He hadn't destroyed his house on purpose.

Sure, said Huk, that's easy for *you* to say. Whether Grasshopper did this on purpose or not doesn't really matter — Worm's house was wrecked.

That's true, but the tale still has a pretty good ending, Tuk said, because after Worm's house was gone, he climbed up an apple tree in order to get a new house. The tree was full of apples and Worm could choose which apple would become his new house.

Even before his house was completely destroyed, Worm had mentioned to Grasshopper that he needed a new house because the old house had a hole in the roof. They both laughed at that and felt a little better about the situation.

Things did get way out of hand, Huk said, but Grasshopper did what he could, and Worm realized that. I guess that makes a difference somehow. If Grasshopper had simply ignored what happened after he had taken a bite out of Worm's house, Worm would probably have been really angry.

I would have been furious that my house was destroyed, Tuk said, even if Grasshopper didn't intend to do it.

Hmm, Huk replied, I guess I could be mad or upset, but not at Grasshopper. I mean Grasshopper already feels bad, and Worm didn't want to make him feel any worse.

It's a tough situation, Tuk conceded, I'll give you that. I'm glad Worm found a new house; otherwise, he may not have been so nice to Grasshopper.

I know, Huk agreed. And what's more, if you think about it, something good came out of it too — a new home without a hole in the roof even.

Isn't it interesting, Tuk said, how things that look one way — and in this case it didn't look very good — can turn out yet another way completely! And in this case, they even turned out for the better.

How to face the ultimate loss of control

— *Duck, Death and the Tulip* by Wolf Erlbruch —

Huk thought about how sometimes things can happen in life that we never expect to happen and how we usually just go about our daily lives not giving things much thought. For instance, Huk thought, Grasshopper had no idea that eating a bite out of the apple would result in destroying Worm's house.

After Huk shared these thoughts with Tuk, Tuk looked solemnly at Huk and said, And sometimes death is what we least expect.

Huk shuddered. Huk had not thought about death at all.

Shaken by Tuk's remark, Huk said, Actually, I know a beautiful tale about death and how it can come so unexpectedly.

Tuk, have you heard the tale about Duck, Death and the tulip?

No, replied Tuk, but I would like to hear it if it is a beautiful tale, as you say.

Well, Huk began, Duck used to live near the pond, close to the apple trees down below my house.

Duck went about her daily life being a duck. One day she suddenly noticed that something was behind her, so she looked around.

She saw someone and asked, Who are you?

I am Death, the someone answered. So you finally noticed me.

Duck, of course, was completely taken off guard and scared stiff. She asked Death whether he was coming to fetch her.

Oh no, Death replied, I'm really always close by. But usually nobody notices me.

So, what happened when Duck realized Death had been close by all along? Tuk asked.

Well, Huk said, Death added that he was always close by — *just in case* — whereupon Duck asked, just in case *what*? I guess Duck was still scared, Huk added, and didn't trust Death at all.

In case something happens to you, Death replied, a nasty cold or an accident.

Are you going to *make* something happen? Duck asked.

And again, Huk said, Death came with a very interesting answer. First, he responded that he is *always* close by, and then he replied that it is *life* that takes care of that, the coughs and colds and whatever happens to you.

And think about it, Huk said, we always think death is making these things happen, but it's life really. Life happens and life is full of illnesses and accidents and everything else that happens to us. Death is close by *just in case*, but life makes things happen.

Death, Huk concluded, is actually really nice. He is not what we often make him out to be.

Did Duck think so? Tuk asked.

Yes, Huk replied. Duck slowly started to warm up to Death and even suggested they go to the pond together. Death didn't like the pond much. He didn't like the damp and cold, so once they returned from spending time at the pond, Duck offered to warm him a little and she spread herself over Death's cold body. No one had offered to warm Death up before.

This is a nice tale, Tuk thought. It puts Death in a friendly light. And that is truly reassuring and a reason we might not have to fear him so much.

When Duck and Death woke the next morning, Duck was very happy to be alive. For fun, she poked Death in the ribs, saying, I'm not dead.

That takes nerve, Tuk said, being able to joke around with Death.

Then Duck started to ask Death some questions, Huk continued. Some ducks say, Duck began, that you become an angel looking over the earth, and some ducks say that deep in the earth there is a place where you'll be roasted if you haven't been a good duck. Death responded by simply saying, You ducks come up with some amazing stories, but who knows?

Then Death asked, What shall we do today?

They decided not to go to the pond again but to climb a tree instead.

Duck wondered aloud what it would be like if she were dead. The pond would be alone, she said, alone without me.

Death finished the thought, saying, The pond will be gone too — at least for you.

That made Duck feel uncomfortable.

I would feel uncomfortable, too, said Tuk, and a little scared too. The idea that nothing will be there anymore — at least for me — gives me the shivers. How can there be nothing left at all, all of a sudden? I know things will continue to *exist* without me, but how can I exist without anything around me? This is very confusing. I don't like it.

That's the mystery of death, Huk said, and the mystery of life too, actually.

Tuk was not satisfied and continued to feel uneasy about this whole thing. Wanting a distraction from these unsettling thoughts, Tuk asked Huk to continue with the tale.

When summer was ending, Huk continued, Duck and Death went to the pond less regularly. They often sat together in the grass, saying little.

Then one day Duck felt a chill and was cold. Can you warm me a little? she asked Death.

When the snowflakes started to drift down, Death saw Duck was no longer breathing. She lay quite still.

Tears started to well up in Tuk's eyes.

Huk noticed Tuk's sadness and tried to console Tuk. Huk said, Death stroked Duck's feathers and then carried her to the great river. He put her in the water and laid the tulip on top of her still body. Then he gently nudged her on her way. For a long time, he watched her and thought to himself, But that's life.

Huk and Tuk briefly looked at each other and considered what Death had said.

Tuk broke the silence. You know, maybe we should cherish life more — I mean, *before* we die.

Life and death do go *together*, Huk said, but we usually don't notice Death until we are ready to die.

Then Huk continued, I heard this story from the author of *our* stories. She says that before we came into this world, we were asked if we really wanted to live life on earth. Of course, we quickly replied, yes, of course. But then the follow-up question came, Even if it means that you will have to die? Not thinking twice, we replied again, Of course, yes! So here we are, so eager to live life on earth that we didn't pay much attention to the second half of the bargain — that we would have to die one day. And so, when we walk around like Duck, not assuming anything and finally noticing Death is close by, we are scared stiff, as we remember the bargain we signed on to.

That's an interesting idea, Huk, Tuk said. That may explain why we don't really pay attention to death. We simply forget death is part of life.

When we had our tails, Tuk continued, we were connected to life *and* death. We were connected to everything around us, and, remembering that death is always close by — all the time — we cherished things more.

Are you saying, Huk said, that when we lost our tails, we also lost our connection to death and thought death was not something to take seriously? That it was something we had control over?

Until we find out, Tuk said, that we have no control over death whatsoever.

Huk and Tuk were quiet for a while and marveled at the sunset — a sunset that, they both thought, was even more beautiful after this tale about Duck and Death and the tulip. It was peaceful and it made them feel that the world with all its woes and worries around things that were out of their control was also a place where they could feel at ease and that they could call home.

by Roger Gutierrez

How to rejoice in what is beyond our control

— *Bear and Wolf* by Daniel Salmieri —

A few days later, Huk decided to go outside to see the night sky as it was slowly disappearing. A good time to visit Tuk, Huk thought, and watch the sunrise from Tuk's backyard.

As Huk walked over to Tuk's, Huk thought, It's interesting — if you think about it — that sunset and sunrise are equally beautiful.

When Huk arrived at Tuk's house, Tuk happily joined Huk in saying goodbye to the night sky and saying hello to the new day.

While they watched, Tuk said, I know another tale about two unlikely friends, sort of like Duck and Death.

What tale is that? Huk asked.

It's the tale of Bear and Wolf, said Tuk.

Let me get some hot tea, Tuk said, before I begin

telling this tale. Hot tea goes well with sunrises, but also sunsets really.

Huk agreed, and Tuk headed inside to get some hibiscus tea for both of them.

When Tuk returned, Huk said what was on Huk's mind: Anyone can become friends. We only call friendships unlikely when we think of friends having to be similar, like only bears can be friends with bears and only wolves can be friends with wolves.

Even Duck and Death became friends, Huk added.

Tuk shuddered but agreed, You don't have to be the same to be friends. I think friendship is more about sharing, Tuk said, and Duck and Death did share in each other's company before Duck passed away.

Huk was quiet for a while and then said, smiling, And we are friends who love to share tales with each other — tales and tea. So do continue with your tale, Tuk, about Bear and Wolf.

One day, Tuk started, Bear was walking through a snowy forest when she spotted something through the glistening snow.

by Karlie Arreola

At the same time, Wolf was walking through the glistening snow and spotted something walking toward him.

As they got closer to each other, Bear saw a young wolf with a pointy snout, gray fur and a wet black nose.

Wolf saw the bear's round head, black fur and wet black nose.

Huk smiled. That's cute, Huk said. They both have a wet black nose.

Bear asked Wolf whether he was lost wandering through the forest on his own. And Wolf asked Bear whether she was lost wandering through the forest on her own.

I don't think they are lost, Huk thought. The forest is their home. You can't be lost in your home.

Both Bear and Wolf said that they loved feeling the cold air on their faces and hearing the quiet when it snows.

Can you hear the quiet? Huk wondered aloud.

Bear then told Wolf that she liked to walk through the forest and asked Wolf if he wanted to walk with

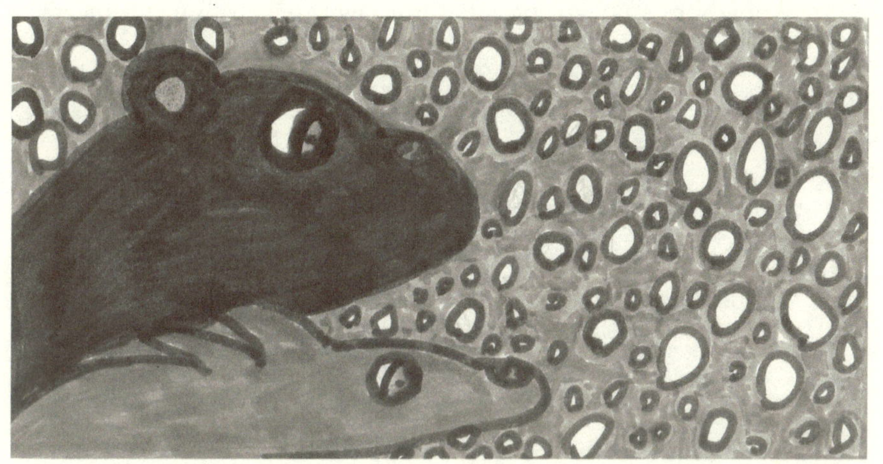

by Roger Gutierrez

her. Sure, Wolf replied. And off they went, walking through the quiet snowy world together.

It sounds a little like Frog and Toad when Frog left Toad a note on his door saying that he wanted to be alone. Remember when Toad finally found Frog sitting alone on the island and how Frog explained how he enjoyed being alone by himself but also enjoyed being alone together with Toad? asked Huk. Maybe Wolf and Bear enjoy being alone together, too.

Perhaps, said Tuk, they enjoy walking through this magical winter land alone together, smelling the wet bark of the trees, hearing the sound of snowflakes falling on their fur.

As they walked, Tuk continued, they suddenly spotted a snowy bird high up in the branches. And then Bird, from way up high, spotted Bear and Wolf down below.

Bird flew down from her branch to get a closer look of these two friends walking side by side through the peaceful and quiet snowy landscape.

As Bear and Wolf were walking alone together, they came upon a clearing in the forest. The clearing was a huge lake, now frozen and covered with snow. After they cleared away some of the snow, they could see fish floating. The fish were asleep deep in the water.

Then Bear told Wolf that she had to get back to her cave where she would sleep through the rest of the winter until springtime when it was time to leave the den.

Then Wolf told Bear that he too had to leave and get back to his wolf pack.

They had loved being in each other's company and now they went their separate ways.

I really liked walking with you, said Bear.

I really liked walking with you, said Wolf. I hope we'll meet again.

They parted ways.

They spent the rest of the winter with their families until spring arrived. The snow had melted. The birds sang in the treetops. The forest burst with life.

And when Bear was walking through the lush green forest, she suddenly saw something through the green grass. It was Wolf.

by Nevaeh Hernandez

And once again, Bear and Wolf took off together.

By the time Tuk had finished this tale, the sun was up and the friends had finished their tea.

Let's take a walk together like Bear and Wolf did, said Huk, and enjoy this incredible place we call home.

Tuk agreed and said, Isn't it interesting to think — referring to the tale of Duck, Death and the tulip — that death is not the end life, but perhaps the other way around, that life continues even after death, sort of how spring follows winter all over again? That's what I like about this tale, because after the cold winter, spring comes back and everything is full of life once again.

And that's life, Huk said with a big smile.

Tuk agreed, That's life.

References

Erlbruch, *Wolf. Duck, Death and the Tulip*. Trans. Catherine Chidgey. New Zealand: English Translation Gecko Press, 2008.

Lobel, Arnold. "Dragons and Giants," in *Frog and Toad Together*. New York: HarperCollins Publishers, 1971.

——. "The Garden," in *Frog and Toad Together*. New York: HarperCollins Publishers, 1971.

——. "A New House," in *Grasshopper on the Road*. New York: HarperCollins Publishers, 1978.

Salmieri, Daniel. *Bear and Wolf*. New York: Enchanted Lion Books, 2018.

Acknowledgements

I would like to acknowledge the elementary school students at El Toyon Elementary School in San Diego, California, whose drawings are the illustrations for this series. For three years prior to the COVID-19 pandemic, I conducted in-person classes in philosophy with students at El Toyon in the first, second and third grades. I began each class by reading a picture book, then students spent time thinking about the questions that came up for them and discussed these questions in small groups. Finally, they wrote down their thoughts about the story and drew pictures. They considered, for example, that when on a life journey together, friends such as Bear and Wolf do not have to be the same to be friends. In fact, life becomes more interesting when friends bring such different life perspectives to a friendship.

During those three years, I worked with teachers Yen Dang, Silvia Toledo, Patricia Carrillo, Pat Duran and Elizabeth McEvoy. I am thankful to these teachers for their dedication to doing philosophy with children and for encouraging the students to think for themselves. During the COVID-19 lockdowns and restrictions, I continued working on the series with Patricia Carrillo and Yen Dang, who would do read-alouds of the stories and ask the children to explore the important questions they brought up when I couldn't be present in the classroom.

I want to thank the students for the use of their drawings as illustrations in the books, as well as their parents who gave their permission to use them. I am very grateful that we were able to continue the Huk and Tuk series in spite of the additional pressure the teachers and parents had to cope with during the pandemic.

Once again, I am always grateful for the feedback from my friend and colleague Claartje van Sijl and, of course, from Mr. Lizzard.

Finally, thank you to Iguana Books, especially its publisher, Meghan Behse, Cheryl Hawley, and my editor, Holly Warren, who has been a delight to work with. If anyone gets what Huk and Tuk are about, it's Holly.

Maria daVenza Tillmanns

Maria teaches a "Philosophy with Children" program in underserved San Diego schools in partnership with the University of California, San Diego. In 1980, she attended Dr. Matthew Lipman's workshop on philosophy for children and later wrote her dissertation on philosophical counseling and teaching under the direction of Martin Buber scholar Dr. Maurice Friedman. She has publications in a number of international journals. For Maria, philosophy is an art form, and she enjoys painting with ideas. Philosophy has helped her navigate the world in all its complexity, including having a multicultural background and having been raised in the US as well as in the Netherlands. She came back to the US to study and moved across the Atlantic multiple times.

www.ingramcontent.com/pod-product-compliance
Lightning Source LLC
LaVergne TN
LVHW051020080826
845145LV00009B/2724

* 9 7 8 1 7 7 1 8 0 6 2 3 7 *